Prophesying Over Your Mind

Prophetess Georgia Horton

Copyright © 2025 by Georgia Horton
Los Angeles
All rights reserved.
Printed and Bound in the United States of America

Published And Distributed By
Professional Publishing House LLC
1425 W. Manchester Ave. Ste B
Los Angeles, California 90047
323-750-3592
Email: professionalpublishinghouse@yahoo.com
www.Professionalpublishinghouse.com

First printing July 2025
978-1-7328982-9-5
10987654321

No part of this book may be reproduced, stored in a retrieval system, or transmitted in any form or by any means without the prior written permission of the publisher—except by a reviewer who may quote brief passages in a review to be printed in a newspaper, magazine, or journal. For inquiries, contact the publisher: professionalpublishinghouse@yahoo.com.

Dedications

I give all glory and honor to God, the Author and Finisher of my faith. With heartfelt thanks, I acknowledge the individuals who made this work possible.

Leilani Dexter, there are no words that can fully express my heart toward you. From the moment God brought you into my life, you have been cheering me on, supporting every vision, and working in the ministry to make dreams a reality. My prayer for you is that God grants you a double portion for the labor of love you have planted in the field. My Sister-in-Christ, know that the best is yet to come.

Dr. Betty Price, my heart is overflowed with joy from your support of purchasing 100 books. You have always loved, encouraged, and prayed for me. There hasn't been a moment, even during your own struggles, that you didn't take time out to listen. I pray that God continues to bless you. I love you, Mighty Woman of God!

Dr. Fredrick Price Jr., I thank God for your leadership as a mighty man of God. You have poured into my life like a shepherd tending to his sheep. Your support for the work that God has placed in my hands cannot be measured. I will always be grateful and honor the anointing on your life.

Sister Patricia Owens, I thank God for bringing you into my life. You have been a blessing to me. I pray God will continue to use you in His kingdom.
Blessings Forever!

Introduction

Let this mind be in you. Yes, this mind—my thoughts for you, my heart toward you. Thoughts located within the brain, specifically in the cerebral cortex, where complex neural activity generates thought processes.

The brain is a physical organ where thoughts are generated and processed. Thoughts arise from the intricate interplay of billions of neurons communicating through electrical and chemical signals.

Past experiences and memories stored in the brain play a significant role in shaping our thoughts and influencing how we perceive the world.

Now, can you begin to see why I'm concerned about your thoughts? It's only through the revelation produced by my Spirit that you can fully understand who I am and who you are.

In order to mirror my ways, you have to mirror my thoughts. Be not conformed to this world, but be ye transformed by the renewing of your mind.

Be transformed by the blueprint of my unique design for your life. Yes! I have a whole blueprint.
Are you ready?

You are so important to me that I even know the number of hairs on your head even though your hair follicles fall 50-100 times per day!
Luke 12:7

Yes, the very hairs on your head are numbered. Fear not! My beloved one, allow me to reveal to you the vision I have for your life. I have tailor-made a unique way to communicate my desire for you to showcase my glory through you. No one can display my glory in the way I have uniquely designed and placed within you. Just as no two stars or thumbprints are the same, there is only one person created exactly like you my son/daughter. Let this mind be in you, which is also in me, so that you may display your unique vessel. There are many gifts inside of you that the world needs!

"But first"

I need you to bring your mind to the altar.

Do not be conformed to this world: but be ye transformed by the renewing of your mind that ye may prove what is that good, and acceptable, and perfect, will of God.

Amen

Romans 12:2 KJV

For the next 21 days come away with me.

I'm waiting.

Table of Contents

Day 1: Emotional Discipline	2
Day 2: Equanimity	8
Day 3: Non-Judgmentalism	14
Day 4: Faith	20
Day 5: Love	26
Day 6: Communication	32
Day 7: Positiveness	38
Day 8: Honesty	44
Day 9: Presentness	50
Day 10: Empathy	56
Day 11: Flexibility	62
Day 12: Balance	68
Day 13: Responsibility	74
Day 14: Mental Discipline	80
Day 15: Objectivity	86
Day 16: Open-Mindedness	92
Day 17: Appreciation	98
Day 18: Courage	104
Day 19: Egalitarianism	110
Day 20: Assertiveness	116
Day 21: Awareness	122
Afterword	127
Acknowledgements	129

Instructions

For the next 21 days, find a quiet private place or space that you can make an altar for you & God to commune.

Sanctify that space. Make sure the only time there is your time with God.

Also, wash your hands before you go into that space, then anoint both your hands & head with oil.

As you decide what time you're doing your concentration time with your father, whether it's morning, noon, or night, make it when you have a clear 4 hours. Be sure to fast for the full four hours from food & social media. Your 4 hours should be inclusive of reading and meditation. You can sit and meditate, go for a walk, exercise, etc. Just no food or social media for those 4 hours.

Welcome to

Prophesying Over Your Mind!

21 Days

Day 1

Be anxious for nothing, but in everything by prayer and supplication, with thanksgiving, let your requests be made known to God; and the peace of God, which surpasses all understanding, will guard your hearts and minds through Christ Jesus.

Philippians 4:6-7 NKJV

Emotional Discipline

Emotional Discipline is the ability to forgo gratification and to refrain from volatile emotions and mood swings.

When this discipline is underdeveloped, we tend to exhibit impulsive behavior and typically pursue immediate gratification. This can take the form of satisfying a desire or avoiding discomfort. It is also difficult for someone to follow rules, procedures, or to reason clearly if our emotions pull us in a different direction.

When our emotions are functioning effectively, we exhibit control over our emotions and desires and readily forgo immediate gratification or endure present discomfort if a greater benefit can be obtained by doing so.

Self-Reflection

As you self-reflect, can you identify these attributes surfacing at times?

Remember this is between you and God. No one will see your response unless you share it.

On the next few pages write out your thoughts, emotions, and answers. After you have finished processing, pray the Prophecy Prayer over your mind.

Prophecy Prayer

To start, inhale for four seconds, hold for seven seconds, then exhale for eight seconds. Repeat this as many times as you need to relax and dissociate from everything around you and anything that is irrelevant on your mind.

Lord,

    I believe that You have supplied all my needs by Your riches in glory through Christ Jesus.
    I believe You have gone before me and made every crooked road straight, so I rest in You. I will not be anxious about anything, but in everything, through prayer and supplication, I will let my requests be made known to You. I trust You.

Amen

Day 2

Thou wilt keep him in perfect peace, whose mind is stayed on thee:
because he trusteth in thee.

Isaiah 26:3 KJV

Equanimity

Equanimity is an equal-minded acceptance of all circumstances and the recognition of the intrinsic value of all things.

When underdeveloped, every event and circumstance is judged as either good or bad.

When functioning properly, we are able to loosen our personal expectations of reality and accept circumstances and the behavior of others as they are, without judging them by what we believe should or should not have happened. We receive with equal-minded acceptance both easy circumstances and difficult ones. We are able to accept the things we cannot control and respond to both insults and flattery with even-mindedness.

Self-Reflection

As you self-reflect, can you identify these attributes surfacing at times?

Remember this is between you and God. No one will see your response unless you share it.

On the next few pages write out your thoughts, emotions, and answers. After you have finished processing, pray the Prophecy Prayer over your mind.

Prophecy Prayer

To start, inhale for four seconds, hold for seven seconds, then exhale for eight seconds. Repeat this as many times as you need to relax and dissociate from everything around you and anything that is irrelevant on your mind.

Lord,

I give You total control of my equanimity.
You are my strong tower, my anchor. I bring all my concerns at Your feet, fully persuaded that You are Lord of all.
Keep me calm and balanced as I walk through the cares of life, knowing I can cast them on You because You care for me.
Thank You for keeping my mind in perfect peace, because I keep my mind on You.
your Daughter/Son,

Amen

Day 3

Judge not, and ye shall not be judged: condemn not, and ye shall not be condemned: forgive, and ye shall be forgiven: give, and it shall be given unto you.

Luke 6:37-38 KJV

Non-Judgmentalism

Non-judgmentalism is the ability and practice of not making conclusions and judgments about people based on their thoughts, beliefs, motives, or actions.

When underdeveloped, we readily adopt critical conclusions and opinions of others. We put faith in our judgments about the thoughts, actions, and beliefs of others and readily assume and assign ill motives to them.

When functioning effectively, we decline to find fault in others and accept mistakes, as well as less-than-perfect beliefs and actions, as a normal and understandable part of human life that everyone struggles with.

Self-Reflection

As you self-reflect, can you identify these attributes surfacing at times?

Remember this is between you and God. No one will see your response unless you share it.

On the next few pages write out your thoughts, emotions, and answers. After you have finished processing, pray the Prophecy Prayer over your mind.

Prophecy Prayer

To start, inhale for four seconds, hold for seven seconds, then exhale for eight seconds. Repeat this as many times as you need to relax and dissociate from everything around you and anything that is irrelevant on your mind.

Lord,

    I thank You that You love me with unconditional love. That You don't judge me but correct me in love and guide me in Your ways.

    I ask You to help me overcome every judgmental way and thought I have toward my sisters and brothers. Help me to see them the way You see them. Teach them to see me the way You see me.

    Lord, I will judge not, so I will not be judged. I will not condemn, and I will not be condemned. Give, Lord, that I may be given to.

Amen

Day 4

Now faith is the substance of things hoped for, the evidence of things not seen.

Hebrews 11:1 KJV

Faith

Faith is the ability to be confident that events and circumstances contain within themselves opportunities for the betterment of the individual.

When underdeveloped, we live in constant anxiety about what is going to occur or not occur in our lives.

When functioning effectively, we are able to confidently trust that whatever comes to pass will provide opportunities for our benefit. We can recognize those opportunities, capitalize on them, and be appreciative of them.

Self-Reflection

As you self-reflect, can you identify these attributes surfacing at times?

Remember this is between you and God. No one will see your response unless you share it.

On the next few pages write out your thoughts, emotions, and answers. After you have finished processing, pray the Prophecy Prayer over your mind.

Prophecy Prayer

To start, inhale for four seconds, hold for seven seconds, then exhale for eight seconds. Repeat this as many times as you need to relax and dissociate from everything around you and anything that is irrelevant on your mind.

Lord,

    I thank You that You are a God who meets me where I'm at. That if I have faith as small as a mustard seed, I can move obstacles as long as that faith is rooted in You and Your Word.

    Lord, increase my faith in You and remove any doubts that may be in my heart. I believe in Your Word, God, and I trust in You. I know faith is the substance of everything I need and the evidence of what is to come into my life.

Amen

Day 5

Beloved, let us love one another: for love is of God; and every one that loveth is born of God, and knoweth God. He that loveth not knoweth not God: for God is love.
1 John 4:7-8 KJV

Love

Love is one of the most confusing words in the english language. Love as one of the indices of consciousness, love is perhaps more clearly stated as "selfless love." It represents a free gift from the heart without expectation of anything in return. It is the ability to see and value all people's needs and happiness as equally important to our own.

When underdeveloped, we exhibit a total lack of concern for anyone's welfare or needs other than our own. Whenever we give or make sacrifices for others, it is with the conscious or subconscious expectation that the favor will be returned.

When this attribute is functioning effectively, we exhibit the same concern for others as much as our limits and responsibilities allow—as we do for ourselves.

Self-Reflection

As you self-reflect, can you identify these attributes surfacing at times?

Remember this is between you and God. No one will see your response unless you share it.

On the next few pages write out your thoughts, emotions, and answers. After you have finished processing, pray the Prophecy Prayer over your mind.

Prophecy Prayer

To start, inhale for four seconds, hold for seven seconds, then exhale for eight seconds. Repeat this as many times as you need to relax and dissociate from everything around you and anything that is irrelevant on your mind.

Lord,

    I thank You that You love me and continue to bestow upon me Your grace and mercy. Teach me how to love the way You love. I want to be an instrument of Your grace and mercy to the world.
    I thank You that even now, You are pouring Your love into my heart and soul. I understand that love is from You and a sign to the world that we are Your children.

Amen

Day 6

The tongue has the power of life and death, and those who love it will eat its fruits.

Proverbs 18:21 NIV

Communication

Communication is the ability to convey to others an accurate picture of what we are thinking or feeling, and to obtain a clear understanding of what others are thinking or feeling.

When underdeveloped, we may have difficulty listening to or truly understanding what another person is trying to express. We may also struggle to effectively convey our own thoughts or feelings.

When this attribute is functioning effectively, we are skilled at both sending and receiving accurate information. This is not to say that miscommunication never occurs, but it happens much less frequently and when it does, we are quick to recognize and correct it.

Self-Reflection

As you self-reflect, can you identify these attributes surfacing at times?

Remember this is between you and God. No one will see your response unless you share it.

On the next few pages write out your thoughts, emotions, and answers. After you have finished processing, pray the Prophecy Prayer over your mind.

Prophecy Prayer

To start, inhale for four seconds, hold for seven seconds, then exhale for eight seconds. Repeat this as many times as you need to relax and dissociate from everything around you and anything that is irrelevant on your mind.

Lord,

    Teach me to communicate what I think and feel effectively, so my words will be in step with Your will for my life and for those I come in contact with.

    I desire for my words to align with what You have predestined. I understand that death and life are in the power of the tongue, so I speak blessings over my life today and over my loved ones.

Amen

Day 7

Let the words of my mouth, and the meditation of my heart, be acceptable in thy sight, oh Lord, my strength, and my redeemer.
Psalms 19:14 NIV

Positiveness

Positiveness is the ability to view positive aspects and possibilities within any given situation and to refrain from negative words, thoughts, and actions.

When underdeveloped, we approach situations with the assumption that there is something bad or negative in everything, and we dwell on that aspect. We constantly focus on how things could or should have been.

When this attribute is functioning effectively, we seek out and find the positive aspects of every situation.

Self-Reflection

As you self-reflect, can you identify these attributes surfacing at times?

Remember this is between you and God. No one will see your response unless you share it.

On the next few pages write out your thoughts, emotions, and answers. After you have finished processing, pray the Prophecy Prayer over your mind.

Prophecy Prayer

To start, inhale for four seconds, hold for seven seconds, then exhale for eight seconds. Repeat this as many times as you need to relax and dissociate from everything around you and anything that is irrelevant on your mind.

Lord,

With so many changes going on in the world, sometimes it's hard to stay positive. I know I should be grateful for the things you have given me. Your blessings overflow in my life. The cares of the world get heavy sometimes, and my eyes stop looking to you and focus on my circumstances.

Teach me to give thanks in all things. I speak a merry heart over my life. I cast my fears and worries to you. Thank you for your protection.

Amen

Day 8

Better is the poor that walketh in his integrity, than he that is perverse in his lips, and is a fool.

Proverbs 19:1 KJV

Honesty

Honesty is perhaps the most important and at times, the most painful of the indices. It is the commitment to see, accept, and speak the truth.

When this attribute is underdeveloped, dishonesty is seen as a legitimate means to achieve desired ends.

When it is fully developed, we strive to be honest with ourselves, no matter how painful it may be, and we are honest with all people.

Self-Reflection

As you self-reflect, can you identify these attributes surfacing at times?

Remember this is between you and God. No one will see your response unless you share it.

On the next few pages write out your thoughts, emotions, and answers. After you have finished processing, pray the Prophecy Prayer over your mind.

Prophecy Prayer

To start, inhale for four seconds, hold for seven seconds, then exhale for eight seconds. Repeat this as many times as you need to relax and dissociate from everything around you and anything that is irrelevant on your mind.

Lord,

    I know it's hard sometimes to be honest. Teach me not to have a spirit of fear when I'm faced with challenges that require me to be truthful. Give me the courage to speak the truth in love. I thank You now that Your Spirit is being poured out on me. I aim to please You by walking in integrity.

Amen

Day 9

Therefore, do not worry about tomorrow, for tomorrow will worry about itself. Each day has enough trouble of its own.

Matthew 6:34 NIV

Presentness

Presentness is the ability to remain focused and centered in the here and now.

When this attribute is underdeveloped, we are constantly preoccupied with the past or the future.

When this attribute is functioning effectively, we remain centered in and focused on the present, making the most of what exists in our here and now.

Self-Reflection

As you self-reflect, can you identify these attributes surfacing at times?

Remember this is between you and God. No one will see your response unless you share it.

On the next few pages write out your thoughts, emotions, and answers. After you have finished processing, pray the Prophecy Prayer over your mind.

Prophecy Prayer

To start, inhale for four seconds, hold for seven seconds, then exhale for eight seconds. Repeat this as many times as you need to relax and dissociate from everything around you and anything that is irrelevant on your mind.

Lord,

    Help me to receive each day what You have for me—to be fully present in the day You've blessed me to see. I know that sometimes I worry about the future or get stuck in my past.
    Teach me to receive my daily bread each day. You said Your mercy is new every morning, and I believe in Your faithfulness. Teach me not to worry about tomorrow. I speak peace over my life and rest in Your plans.

Amen

Day 10

Be kind and compassionate to one another, forgiving each other, just as in Christ God forgave you.

Ephesians 4:32 NIV

Empathy

Empathy is the ability to place oneself in another's position and to see and feel things from their perspective.

When this attribute is underdeveloped, we think only from our own point of view and focus on how things impact us.

When this attribute is functioning effectively, we can easily and with a good degree of accuracy, perceive the thoughts and feelings another person may be experiencing at a given time.

Moreover, we respect the other person's perspective and feelings and can often sense and feel any emotional pain they may be experiencing.

Self-Reflection

As you self-reflect, can you identify these attributes surfacing at times?

Remember this is between you and God. No one will see your response unless you share it.

On the next few pages write out your thoughts, emotions, and answers. After you have finished processing, pray the Prophecy Prayer over your mind.

Prophecy Prayer

To start, inhale for four seconds, hold for seven seconds, then exhale for eight seconds. Repeat this as many times as you need to relax and dissociate from everything around you and anything that is irrelevant on your mind.

Lord,

I thank You for every time You've forgiven me and shown me grace and mercy. I cannot count the times I have fallen and come short of Your glory.
Teach me to show that same mercy and grace to others, so they may experience Your love. Pour more of Your love into my heart, that I may show others Your tender mercy.

Amen

Day 11

I do everything to spread the Good News and share in its blessings.

1 Corinthians 9:23 NLT

Flexibility

Flexibility is the ability to accept change and adapt to new or unexpected circumstances.

When this attribute is underdeveloped, we find it difficult to cope with or accept things that differ from our habits or expectations.

When this attribute is functioning effectively, we are able to flow with whatever course circumstances may take, regardless of how much things deviate from what we expected. We accept and make the most of whatever comes. We frequently exhibit and enjoy the benefits of innovative and creative approaches to circumstances and events, and we are open to recognizing and capitalizing on the opportunities they offer.

Self-Reflection

As you self-reflect, can you identify these attributes surfacing at times?

Remember this is between you and God. No one will see your response unless you share it.

On the next few pages write out your thoughts, emotions, and answers. After you have finished processing, pray the Prophecy Prayer over your mind.

Prophecy Prayer

To start, inhale for four seconds, hold for seven seconds, then exhale for eight seconds. Repeat this as many times as you need to relax and dissociate from everything around you and anything that is irrelevant on your mind.

Lord,

      Sometimes I want to do things my way. My flesh doesn't want to bend to what I know is true and good for me. I can be difficult in my viewpoints and resist seeing things from other perspectives.

      Teach me to be flexible toward those around me. Help me to see and understand things from their point of view. I speak a submissive spirit over my life and release the spirit of stubbornness. Thank You for giving me Your understanding.

Amen

Day 12

Let your moderation be known unto all men. The Lord is at hand.

Philippians 4:5 KJV

Balance

Balance is the ability to pursue moderation while avoiding extremes. It is the judicious harmonizing of opposites.

When this attribute is underdeveloped, a person will be drawn into extremes of view, belief, or action. This can manifest as overindulgence or addictive behavior.

When functioning effectively, a person will balance or blend traits of apparent polar opposites. Many wisdom traditions hold that the path of individual growth involves balancing the masculine and feminine energies within each person. Justice and principle, and pragmatism are just a few examples of the dualities that people constantly strive to balance and harmonize.

Self-Reflection

As you self-reflect, can you identify these attributes surfacing at times?

Remember this is between you and God. No one will see your response unless you share it.

On the next few pages write out your thoughts, emotions, and answers. After you have finished processing, pray the Prophecy Prayer over your mind.

Prophecy Prayer

To start, inhale for four seconds, hold for seven seconds, then exhale for eight seconds. Repeat this as many times as you need to relax and dissociate from everything around you and anything that is irrelevant on your mind.

Lord,

     Sometimes I can become unbalanced on some issues. I know that allowing this attribute to run wild in this area can affect other areas of my life, as well as the people around me. I understand it can also affect my day-to-day activities.

     I ask that You teach me how to be balanced in You. I speak balance to my spirit, thoughts, and emotions. Thank You for bringing my spirit in line with Your Word.

Amen

Day 13

But he that knew not, and did not commit things worthy of stripes, shall be beaten worth few stripes. For unto whomsoever much is given, of him shall be much required: and to whom men have commited, much of him they will ask more.

Luke 12:48 KJV

Responsibility

Responsibility is the willingness, ability, and actuality of people accepting their role in the positive and negative consequences that flow from their actions and inaction.

When underdeveloped, we try to blame less-than-optimal circumstances on other people, events—anything other than ourselves.

When this attribute is functioning effectively, we readily take on challenges and tasks appropriate for us; we accept the blame and the obligation to make repairs, improvements, or meet demands if we have contributed to less-than-ideal circumstances.
Furthermore, we have no qualms about being held accountable for our actions and decisions.

Self-Reflection

As you self-reflect, can you identify these attributes surfacing at times?

Remember this is between you and God. No one will see your response unless you share it.

On the next few pages write out your thoughts, emotions, and answers. After you have finished processing, pray the Prophecy Prayer over your mind.

Prophecy Prayer

To start, inhale for four seconds, hold for seven seconds, then exhale for eight seconds. Repeat this as many times as you need to relax and dissociate from everything around you and anything that is irrelevant on your mind.

Lord,

    I thank You for the things You have blessed me with and entrusted to me. I want to be a faithful servant over all that You have given me—my children, wife, husband, money, friendships, talents and most of all my relationship with You.

    Teach me to be responsible over what You have placed into my hands. I speak the spirit of wisdom over my life. I speak blessings and increase in all areas of my life.

Amen

Day 14

Finally, brothers and sisters, whatever is true, whatever is noble, whatever is right, whatever is pure, whatever is lovely, whatever is admirable --- if anything is excellent or praiseworthy – thinks about such things.

Philippians 4:8 NIV

Mental Discipline

Mental discipline is the ability to control one's thoughts. When one is not preoccupied with external stimuli, the mind has a tendency to race and wander.

When this attribute is underdeveloped, we allow random, counterproductive, and even destructive streams of thought to flow through our minds; we are often unaware of many of them.

When functioning effectively, we are continuously aware of the thoughts that arise in our mind, and we control our thinking. Destructive thoughts are discontinued, and mental energy is rerouted to constructive thoughts. When this skill is well developed, we have the ability to stop our thoughts altogether in complete silence.

Self-Reflection

As you self-reflect, can you identify these attributes surfacing at times?

Remember this is between you and God. No one will see your response unless you share it.

On the next few pages write out your thoughts, emotions, and answers. After you have finished processing, pray the Prophecy Prayer over your mind.

Prophecy Prayer

To start, inhale for four seconds, hold for seven seconds, then exhale for eight seconds. Repeat this as many times as you need to relax and dissociate from everything around you and anything that is irrelevant on your mind.

Lord,

    I know that at times I allow my thoughts to wander into places that are not healthy or wise. Sometimes, my thoughts are negative toward others, and in my mind, I judge and criticize people who think, dress, or act differently than I do.

    Teach me to control my thoughts toward others so that I may be a better example to my community and loved ones. I speak over my mind to think true, pure, noble, right, and lovely thoughts. Thank You, Lord, for pouring Your Spirit upon me.

                      Amen

Day 15

And we know that all things work together for good to them that love God, to them who are called according to his purpose.

Romans 8:28 KJV

Objectivity

Objectivity is the ability to see things from different perspectives and to take a position against oneself.

When this attribute is underdeveloped, we see things only from our own point of view. We are unable to step outside ourselves and assess situations from a neutral perspective. In our minds, we are always right.

When this attribute is functioning effectively, we are able to separate our minds from our history and assumptions and see things with "fresh eyes." We readily recognize and accept errors in our thinking or behavior and have no trouble apologizing when we are wrong.

Self-Reflection

As you self-reflect, can you identify these attributes surfacing at times?

Remember this is between you and God. No one will see your response unless you share it.

On the next few pages write out your thoughts, emotions, and answers. After you have finished processing, pray the Prophecy Prayer over your mind.

Prophecy Prayer

To start, inhale for four seconds, hold for seven seconds, then exhale for eight seconds. Repeat this as many times as you need to relax and dissociate from everything around you and anything that is irrelevant on your mind.

Lord,

I know my ability to see is hindered—sometimes by my own self-defeating thoughts and prejudiced thinking. In certain circumstances, it's hard for me to be objective, even when I know I am being difficult.

Teach me to surrender my desire to have things my way and help me see the beauty in different thoughts and ideas. I speak and surrender my spirit unto You, God. Mold me according to Your Word. I take comfort knowing that all things work together for good to those who love You.

Amen

Day 16

Keep your heart with all diligence.
For out of it spring the issues of life.

Proverbs 4:23 NKJV

Open-Mindedness

Open-mindedness is the ability to consider new and different ideas, perspectives, and ways of thinking.

When this attribute is underdeveloped, we feel annoyed or even threatened by ideas, perspectives, or experiences that are new to us.

When this attribute is functioning effectively, we experience no discomfort in exploring new ideas, concepts, and approaches. Although we may not adopt them as our own, we readily give them due consideration.

Moreover, we are comfortable with people who hold belief systems different from our own, and we can accept that those beliefs may hold validity and benefit for others, even if not for ourselves.

Self-Reflection

As you self-reflect, can you identify these attributes surfacing at times?

Remember this is between you and God. No one will see your response unless you share it.

On the next few pages write out your thoughts, emotions, and answers. After you have finished processing, pray the Prophecy Prayer over your mind.

Prophecy Prayer

To start, inhale for four seconds, hold for seven seconds, then exhale for eight seconds. Repeat this as many times as you need to relax and dissociate from everything around you and anything that is irrelevant on your mind.

Lord,

    I want to have a clear mind so I can be a seeker of knowledge, but the knowledge that comes from You. An open mind is like fertile soil—ready to receive the seeds of divine wisdom that God sows.
    Teach me Your ways, O Lord, that I may be a light in this dark world. I speak willingness to receive Your knowledge and wisdom into my mind and heart.
I surrender my thoughts to You.

Amen

Day 17

In everything give thanks: for this is the will of God in Christ Jesus concerning you.

1 Thessalonians 5:18 KJV

Appreciation

Appreciation is the ability to find beauty and value in all things.

When this attribute is underdeveloped, we exhibit a lack of gratitude for what is done for us—even in the greatest acts of charity. We fail to see the inherent beauty and value that exist in things. We focus on what does not meet our preferences and may show indifference or even disrespect toward the people and things in our lives.

When this attribute is functioning effectively, we demonstrate respect and gratitude for everything within our experience. We consistently perceive the intrinsic value in all things and people. We do not take anyone or anything for granted, and we feel a sincere sense of gratitude for all that we experience.

Self-Reflection

As you self-reflect, can you identify these attributes surfacing at times?

Remember this is between you and God. No one will see your response unless you share it.

On the next few pages write out your thoughts, emotions, and answers. After you have finished processing, pray the Prophecy Prayer over your mind.

Prophecy Prayer

To start, inhale for four seconds, hold for seven seconds, then exhale for eight seconds. Repeat this as many times as you need to relax and dissociate from everything around you and anything that is irrelevant on your mind.

Lord,

    I know sometimes I don't show appreciation for the thing you have blessed me with. Sometimes I complain about housework instead of being grateful that I have a roof over my head.

    At times, I complain about my job instead of being thankful that I have one or complain about my family when I should be thankful I am not alone in this world.

    I speak a grateful spirit over my mind. Lord, teach me to be grateful and thankful. Give me a spirit of appreciation.

Amen

Day 18

Have not I commanded thee? Be strong and of a good courage; be not afraid, neither be thou dismayed: for the Lord thy God is with thee whithersover thou goest.

Joshua 1:9 KJV

Courage

Courage is the ability to view fear and emotional pain as helpful markers—indicating where we have the greatest opportunity for growth and then actively pursue that growth.

When this attribute is underdeveloped, we go to great lengths to avoid unfamiliar or uncomfortable circumstances. We forgo growth and personal improvement rather than face emotional pain, discomfort, or our own personal weaknesses.

When this attribute is functioning effectively, we recognize the fears, pains, and personal weaknesses that need to be addressed in order to break their hold and detrimental impact on us. We readily and honestly own, face, and deal with our fears, pains, and discomforts.

Self-Reflection

As you self-reflect, can you identify these attributes surfacing at times?

Remember this is between you and God. No one will see your response unless you share it.

On the next few pages write out your thoughts, emotions, and answers. After you have finished processing, pray the Prophecy Prayer over your mind.

Prophecy Prayer

To start, inhale for four seconds, hold for seven seconds, then exhale for eight seconds. Repeat this as many times as you need to relax and dissociate from everything around you and anything that is irrelevant on your mind.

Lord,

    At times, I see injustice and turn a blind eye or make excuses for not doing anything. There are times I don't even want to face my own personal weaknesses. I know that's a habit I need to break.

    Teach me how to have the courage to make the necessary changes I need for self-improvement. I speak courage over my life to accept the things I can't change and I ask for the wisdom to know the difference. For the things I can change today, I put one foot forward to start with your help.

Amen

Day 19

There is neither Jew nor Gentile, neither slave nor free, nor is there male and female, for you are all one in Christ Jesus.

Galatians 3:28 NIV

Egalitarianism

Egalitarianism is the valuing of all people as equal in worth, irrespective of abilities, achievements, or failures.

When this attribute is underdeveloped, we will constantly weigh one person against another.

When this attribute is fully developed, we are able to appreciate differences in skills such as effort, intellect, and talent, but we do not use those differences to assign value. Instead, we see all people as equally valuable, living human beings.

Self-Reflection

As you self-reflect, can you identify these attributes surfacing at times?

Remember this is between you and God. No one will see your response unless you share it.

On the next few pages write out your thoughts, emotions, and answers. After you have finished processing, pray the Prophecy Prayer over your mind.

Prophecy Prayer

To start, inhale for four seconds, hold for seven seconds, then exhale for eight seconds. Repeat this as many times as you need to relax and dissociate from everything around you and anything that is irrelevant on your mind.

Lord,

I believe in Your Holy Word, that You made us all the same. Sometimes, my actions don't match my beliefs. I fight against my personal stigma and prejudices. Some stemming from past hurts and pains, and some from my cultural upbringing. Either way, they are not pleasing in Your sight.

Teach me to love as You love, my Heavenly Father. I speak release from biased thoughts over my mind, and I submit to Your Spirit to cleanse me of all unrighteousness.

Amen

Day 20

My dear brothers and sisters, take note of this: Everyone should be quick to listen, slow to speak and slow to become angry, because human anger does not produce the righteousness that God desires.

James 1:19-20 NIV

Assertiveness

Assertiveness is the ability to overcome silence, passivity, and inertia, and to speak and act in accordance with who one truly is without going to the opposite extreme of being domineering.

When this attribute is underdeveloped, we will either timidly withdraw—suppressing our true self and desires or go to the opposite extreme of forcing our personal agenda on others during interactions.

When this trait is functioning effectively, we are able, in a balanced way, to fully and tactfully express our desires without putting others on the defensive or forcing our agenda on them.

Self-Reflection

As you self-reflect, can you identify these attributes surfacing at times?

Remember this is between you and God. No one will see your response unless you share it.

On the next few pages write out your thoughts, emotions, and answers. After you have finished processing, pray the Prophecy Prayer over your mind.

Prophecy Prayer

To start, inhale for four seconds, hold for seven seconds, then exhale for eight seconds. Repeat this as many times as you need to relax and dissociate from everything around you and anything that is irrelevant on your mind.

Lord,

I want to be balanced in You and Your Word. I don't want to be extreme or force my personal agenda on others. I don't want the authority, power, title, or favor You have blessed me with to be misused toward others. I want to have a meek spirit—humble, so that others may see my good works and glorify You.

Teach me how to show Your love and patience toward others. I speak Your love, Your peace, and Your longsuffering over my life.

Amen

Day 21

Examine yourselves to see whether you are in the faith; test yourselves. Do you not realize that Christ Jesus is in you— unless of course, you fail the test?

2 Corinthians 13:5 NIV

Awareness

Awareness is the ability to consciously recognize the emotions and thoughts that we experience as we experience them.

When this attribute is underdeveloped, we are frequently driven by our subconscious mind, leading us to experience thoughts and feelings without understanding what caused them. Being unaware of what brought these into being, we lack the ability to modify our thinking and reactions. As a result, we remain trapped in negative ruts that cause us unhappiness and pain.

When this attribute is functioning effectively, we are cognizant of our thoughts and feelings as they arise. Consequently, we are able to recognize and follow the chain of reactions that flow from their causes. As a result, we develop an awareness of the origin of pain and unhappiness and are able to dismantle harmful patterns of thought, freeing ourselves from pain and from counterproductive habits of thought and reaction.

Self-Reflection

As you self-reflect, can you identify these attributes surfacing at times?

Remember this is between you and God. No one will see your response unless you share it.

On the next few pages write out your thoughts, emotions, and answers. After you have finished processing, pray the Prophecy Prayer over your mind.

Prophecy Prayer

To start, inhale for four seconds, hold for seven seconds, then exhale for eight seconds. Repeat this as many times as you need to relax and dissociate from everything around you and anything that is irrelevant on your mind.

Lord,

I know that sometimes I allow my past experiences to govern my mental and emotional state. I allow past thoughts to enter and cause confusion in my decision-making concerning my marriage, children, job, and life.
Teach me to release the unhealthy thoughts that are carried in my subconscious. I want to be healed and have my mind renewed. I want to be transformed by the renewing of my mind. I no longer want to be conformed to this world. I speak of liberation from negative thoughts. Lord, I give You full permission to cleanse my mind from all unrighteousness.

Amen

Congratulations!

Congratulations on completing this 21 day journey! You've shown dedication and consistency day by day, and that's something to be truly proud of. These past 21 days are ground-breaking days to prepare the mind. My hope is for you to leave with an understanding how God identifies the mind and its traits. The mind was designed by God, so every intricate detail has been strategically woven for His glory. God has decided to communicate to you through the Holy spirit by the mind and your heart.

Stay tuned for your next instructions in the next volume!

Acknowledgements

Trinity Broadcasting Network
Day Star
Time Magazine
Bishop T.D. Jakes
Mrs. Angela Evans
Chaplain E. Crain
Apostle I Horton
Pastor G. Oliver
Pastor Jones
Rosie Milligan
Mindy Glaser

May God Bless You.

STATE OF CALIFORNIA – DEPARTMENT OF CORRECTIONS AND REHABILITATION

OFFICE OF OFFENDER SERVICES
LETTER OF CERTIFICATION

1/3/2024

To Whom It May Concern:

    This is to certify that Dr.Georgia Horton is the innovator of 7 therapeutic curricula that initially began being taught in 2007 inside the CDC system. These curriculums were developed to address chronic trauma issues. In 2010, Dr. Horton was interviewed by Dr. Gonzales, the supervisor over CCCMS and the mental health staff. Shortly after, she began teaching and developing trauma based curricula with the Mental Health Department. Her curriculum was utilized twice a week in conjunction with normal group programming. She also taught an additional course throughout the week to the CCCMS program. Her hands-on work and training was overseen by licensed clinical Social Workers.

    Dr. Horton's knowledge includes creating programs and lesson plans for people dealing with depression, anxiety, schizophrenia, drug addiction, alcoholism, stress, cccms, personality disorders, mental health issues, interpersonal groups, etc.

    I not only recommend Dr.Georgia Horton's trauma curriculums, but endorse it for any mental health, self-help development, and or life skills field of study and practice. Her tremendous work has changed thousands of lives! Dr. Horton trauma programs are appropriate for all programs dealing with such causes, and can be tailored based on any given circumstance.

S. Freeman LCSW
Mental Health Department

Prophetess Georgia Horton

has written 7 therapeutic curriculums that delve into the complexity of specific issues.

She has received certificates from the City of Stockton, Senators, Government Officials, a letter from the Congress of the United States House of Representatives Washington, DC, for Pipeline community services. She's appeared as a trauma expert regarding the effects of COVID-19 on Trinity Broadcasting Network(TBN), was featured in TIME Magazine, Daystar and also is a 1st place winner for a Telly award.

"I'm constantly astounded by Ms. Horton's genuine passion to help those traumatized by emotional and mental abuse using her own 14 years of hands-on discovery." - S. Freeman LCSW, Mental Health Department

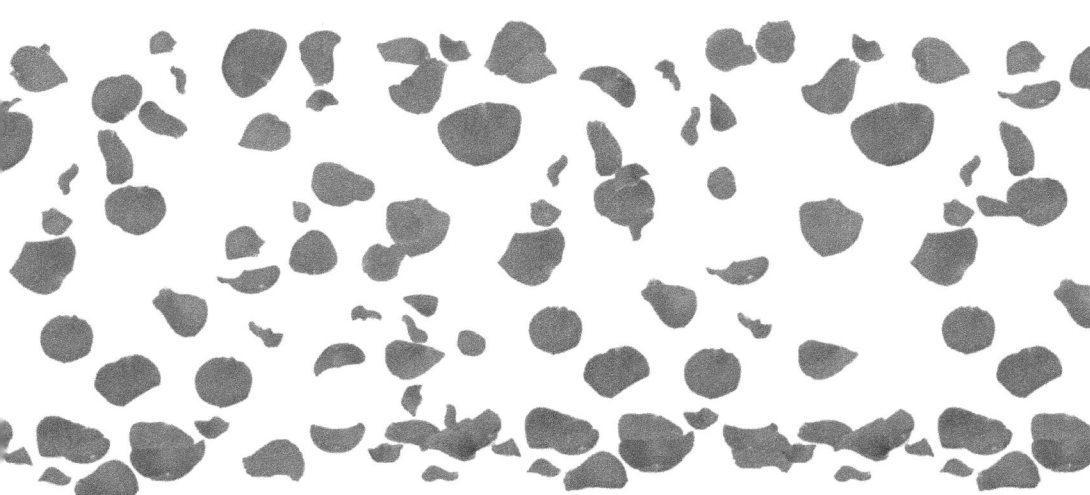

www.ingramcontent.com/pod-product-compliance
Lightning Source LLC
Chambersburg PA
CBHW031150160426
43193CB00008B/321